www.francesstone.ca

A Reflection of Love

A Different Kind of Love Story

by

Frances Stone

Scripture quotations marked KJV are from the Holy Bible,
King James Version (Authorized Version). First published
in 1611. Quoted from the KJV Classic Reference Bible,
Copyright © 1983 by The Zondervan Corporation.

iUniverse books may be ordered through booksellers or by contacting:

iUniverse
1663 Liberty Drive
Bloomington, IN 47403
www.iuniverse.com
1-800-Authors (1-800-288-4677)

ISBN: 978-1-4401-4275-8 (sc)
ISBN: 978-1-4401-4276-5 (e)

Print information available on the last page.

iUniverse rev. date: 10/09/2015

For my mother, for choosing to be mine.

For the hand that rocks the cradle
Is the hand that rules the world

William Ross Wallace

Brad,
Thank you for your
support + kindness.
I truly hope that as
a result of my recovery I'm
able to make a difference in
the world. Thank you for all that
do to make a difference in your
world. All the best,

Mar '21

In Gratitude

To my children, Austin, Aidan and Maya, I thank God for bringing each of you into my life as the individually wrapped gifts that you are, to awaken and expand my heart and faith in such a way that I have become who I am meant to be. I look forward to the pleasure and privilege of spending my entire life watching you grow into the people God created you to be. Although life has not been easy, I would still choose each of you, every single time.

To my first love, thank you for your part in my story. I hope and pray your own story ends well. To my children's father, thank you for the healing of your friendship and for how much and how well you love our children.

And we know that in all things God works for the
good of those who love him, for who have been called
according to his purpose.

February twenty-sixth, 2001

"I didn't do anything wrong," he said defiantly and I felt the hurt in his heart with every word.

My hand strokes his head of beautiful dark brown hair, slowly and gently, as this grown man with his little boy heart lay his head lightly on my stomach. I stop to kiss the top of his head, breathing him in deeply and whisper softly to him, "I know you're going to change my life. I can feel it."

From the corner of the room, set aglow with candlelight, I see the scene and silently applaud for the girl who has finally found what she needs to complete her, love. When he tilts his head up to mine to kiss me gently for saying it, everything in my life, for one glorious moment, is completely still and perfect. I am so loving, peaceful, and changed in a way that I can actually feel, at long last, in my heart.

His name is Luke, and he is tall, with dark-hair and equally dark, mysterious eyes. I am in awe of the simple way he crosses a room, the way his expensive shoes, with their own hard beat, instinctively make me hold my breath, not knowing quite what to expect when he reaches me. He is different from the others, unique and special, and I have been looking for someone just like him for so long, with a heart to which only I hold the key, the key to my own freedom.

We had met on a Sunday, five years earlier, at the grocery store where I work, seeing each other nearly every Sunday after that, when he would come into the store to buy bread and milk. Bread and milk, I would later learn, he neither ate nor drank.

I would smile and make an occasional attempt at a witty remark every time he would show up, my face and neck burning a bright crimson red. One Sunday night, after a particularly long absence, he showed up again and passed me a crumpled note in a nearly illegible scrawl, sweetly asking me to come for a coffee. After calling him, I realized how much we had in common and thinking that was a good thing, suggested we meet for a drink, instead of a coffee.

On the evening of our very first date, my face looks up to the spinning ceiling fan in my kitchen as I stretch my arms wide and spin round and round in my one bedroom suite. While my own picture of cultivated and controlled perfection twists and twirls, my life so far with its pictures of friends, parties and countless books about living your dreams spin around with me, as I try to rid myself of my nerves.

This is my favorite thing, the excitement and anticipation of a date or an evening out, looking for that one moment when my whole life could change, when I will meet the man of my dreams; it is the reality of the man that is usually a disappointment.

I find dating itself a bit of a bore and can hardly stomach the thought of hearing yet another life story from yet another man in which I have no personal interest or investment, but something tells me that this guy might be different and I like different. I used to love different and different loved me back, *but that was then and this is now*—I think, grabbing my car keys and little black evening bag.

February twenty-sixth, 2001

"Finally, a man I don't have to teach how to dress," I joke approvingly, approaching the pool table that Luke stands behind, classically tall and sexy in jeans and a black long-sleeved shirt. Without saying a word in reply, he slowly chalks a pool cue that rests lazily across his heart, as we seduce one another with what is left unsaid until we are ready to leave.

"Frances" he says while I am walking towards the door, having heard my name a thousand times, but only once before in the way that he says it.

For a moment I stand completely still, unable to catch my breath and then slowly turn around to see where he stands tall and beautiful, my little black evening bag held safely in his hands.

I feel the intensity between us as our hands briefly touch, my eyes looking into his for a hint of his next promise, my heart asking for nothing more than this look in his eyes, a look that speaks of the beginning of dreams I'd yet to dream, all at once coming true.

Wanting more of the same, we go back to his apartment where the stage is set with its lights low and the music singing softly, awaiting its audience. Our second act unfolds while I sit at his long, wooden kitchen table, trying to calm the butterflies within me, as I wait to receive the glass of wine that I watch him carefully pour.

I accept his offering, as calm and confident as he, but am disappointed when he sits down at the far end of the table, my mission now to bring down the invisible wall that suddenly lies between us. I begin to open up about myself, asking what I hope are the right questions about him, until finally I achieve my goal and the wall comes down.

He expresses his desire to be honest with me since he has dreamed of me for so long. As I am utterly captivated by his adoration, I listen eagerly and attentively to every single word in the telling of his story.

He speaks the language of his heart, a language my own heart knows and understands, but has yet to hear as he tells me his story. It is a story of a boy that grew into a man in the midst of a broken family with broken hearts, as well as the recent break-up of his marriage of two years, that produced a son of its same age.

"It was different with my son," he says, referring to the way he loved, as he looks up for the first time in the telling of his story, to meet my eyes.

With excitement and pride, he gets up at once from the table where we sit, to retrieve proof of his love, showing me a few gently dog-eared photographs of him with bright eyes and smiling lips carrying an adorable fresh-faced little boy in a backpack in a variety of seasons and landscapes.

I see their smiles when they are at the beach making castles in the sand, and can almost hear their laughter jump from the photograph itself, watching as Daddy crawls around on the floor playing hide 'n' seek in his pajamas in what was once their home, enjoying simple moments of being father and son.

He looks so beautiful, I think to myself, looking at the pictures and then back up at him, wanting to see him smile and laugh like that again.

He tells his side of a story that I can't possibly understand of all the reasons why he left his wife and why their marriage's ending was her fault and not his own. It is a story of power struggles and control issues that extended beyond the marriage, beyond the courtroom and into the life of their two-year-old son.

"So, how do you like me now?" he asks, trying desperately for the air of arrogance he formerly possessed, his slumped shoulders and wilted body that sits much lower in his chair now, telling me a different tale.

My fingers caress the fragile stem of the wine glass as I contemplate this beautiful, confident, sexy man and the wall he has built around his heart. I see all its hurt and pain, the love that it requires now on display before my eyes and my heart runs towards it, instead of away, wanting to help in any way that I can.

"I like you just fine," I reply, feeling up to the challenge and spending the night.

♥

    This moment and this man would begin the purpose and plan for my life, but not in the way that I hoped. Do you believe that all things, good and bad, can be used for a purpose and a plan for your life?

Faith, hope and love.
But the greatest of these is love.

1 Corinthians 13:13

May twenty-first, 1993

Jacob turned the taps off in the shower, tightly, so that no water would escape, grabbing a towel to make sure to dry his body properly, as he had been taught, careful not to forget between his toes. Clean and dry, he felt safe to step on the small, square bathmat strategically placed on the bathroom floor, as he used his towel to wipe away the steam from his hot shower from the small, square mirror above the sink.

He wrapped the clean, white towel firmly around his waist and opened the mirror above the sink to reveal its hidden compartment with its light orange bottles and their white tags, choosing his grandfather's only hair product, Brylcreem, from the bottom shelf, where it always lay on its side, awaiting its next daily use.

With the mirrored door still left ajar, he removed the large white cap from the product and gingerly squeezed its tube, careful to place only a dime-sized amount into the small of his hand. He returned the product precisely to its place on the shelf and closed its door, allowing the chest to keep its secrets.

He entered his room, ignoring the bed with its army tight corners, the dresser with nothing but a lamp on its top and a wall unit that held his music and drawings, but whose light wooden doors, thankfully, hid the mess from sight.

Choosing his favorite black shirt with white skulls and "Skates" emblazoned on its long black sleeves from a neat pile at the top of his closet and baggy brown army pants from the rows of pressed pants on hangers, he dressed quickly, before Mike tired of waiting downstairs with his grandfather.

Finished with his regime, he ran past the bathroom and dashed down the stairs, two steps at a time, to the living room to save Mike, who was laughing loudly at a story about his old army days, that Jacob's grandfather was telling him.

"Goodnight, sir" Jacob said respectfully to his grandfather.

"Goodnight Mike," his grandfather replied coldly, turning his back on Jacob.

"Don't worry man, he'll get over it," Mike told him, referring to Jacob being A.W.O.L. from the army, as they walked together down the long trail of cement steps towards the street where Jacob's dark blue Volkswagen bug, his pride and joy, waited.

"Free alcohol and high school girls at this party tonight, that should cheer you up. Maybe you'll even get lucky for once," he added, giving his friend a playful punch in the arm.

Jacob used his key to unlock the car door as he shook his head, utterly confused by what his grandfather considered a better man.

♥

To remember him was to love him. Do you remember people you loved in your past as an effort to keep them alive in your present?

"Train a child in the way he should go and when he is old he will not turn from it."

Proverbs 22:6

April fifteenth, 2001

The Catholic Church of my childhood stands quietly on a corner, the large cross on its roof and stained glass windows on its side, distinguishing it from any other white painted structure, the paint now a little chipped and dull with the passage of time.

I walk towards it, finding it unassuming and silent in its appearance aside from the tall, heavy wooden doors that guard it. Taking a deep breath, I pull on them and enter with my head held defiantly high, despite my disobedience of the rules these doors contain.

It has been years since I attended, but everything is still very much the same. The long, dark velvet carpeted aisle I walked as a child for my first communion in my pretty white dress with its little gold flecks and matching veil, still looks as far away from the altar as it ever did, its distance now providing a quiet comfort. Standing alone, I am relieved when I finally see my mother and hurry towards the pew in which she sits, waiting patiently despite my late arrival.

Because it is Easter Sunday, I had promised her that I would come and afterwards we are to have lunch together.

12

I'm really here because I have some news to share, but she doesn't know that yet. We hug in greeting, which feels awkward and forced, but we do it anyway in the hope that perhaps one day it won't be.

"When will you be giving me a grandchild, hmmm?" my mother asks me playfully, breaking the silence, her eyes set on the little children playing quietly in the pew before us.

"Careful what you wish for, mother," I answer in a hushed whisper, focusing my gaze straight ahead on the priest.

I am my mother's eleventh child from three prior relationships, upsetting the even five girl, five boy split before me. Upon birth, I became the odd one out. I was raised by her alone, except for short Sunday visits with my father, to always tell the truth and be honest about my sins, regardless of their nature, so that I could be forgiven. Although I didn't understand why she worried so much, for as a child my sins were small. I didn't do anything I would be too embarrassed to confess.

Never disciplined with anything more than disappointment in my mother's eyes, I would always act sorry without ever actually having to say the words, "I'm sorry", waiting for her disappointment to pass and for the forgiveness close behind. I breathed a sigh of relief when I received it, being once again in her good graces. Her grace always good, but her love, a little harder to find.

When I was twelve years old, I asked my mother if I could give her a kiss. She said yes. It was to be our first. I sat on her lap, cupped her face in my hands and asked her to close her eyes while I did the same. Slowly, I tilted my head to the side and leaned in towards her just as I had seen on television. But when I kissed her, instead of receiving her affection as I had hoped, she pushed me off her lap onto the floor, horrified at my attempt, leaving me both embarrassed and confused.

Beneath the vaulted ceiling, the old wooden pews creak and groan in unison as the faithful sit and stand in obedience and attention at the priest's quiet command while a bronzed figure of Jesus Christ nailed to a heavy wooden cross hangs behind him, silently dying for our sins. I am a sinner, of course, but I only think of it the two times a year that I attend church because this world, as safe and familiar to me as it is, is not the real world.

In the real world, I do what people do, what people have always done. I am just like everyone else. I fit in.

The familiar rosewater scent of my mother's hand cream captures my attention and from the corner of my eye, I watch as she rubs it liberally on her hands knowing that she will inevitably take more than she needs, as she always does, and without asking will reach for my hands to gently wipe the excess on me. As she does, her soft, aging hands hold mine just for a moment and as I enjoy the softness of her touch, I feel her love, but don't say a word.

We drive to lunch in my first taste of independence and style, a two-seater, canary yellow convertible sports car. With the top down, the wind blows around us, as we discuss my pregnancy and the new man I've been dating, while both her hands instinctively reach up in an effort to hold her short, dark curly hair in its rightful place.

As my own shoulder-length blonde hair blows wildly in the breeze, the look of love glows within me and can be heard in my every word, as I tell her all about how wonderful he is, we are and I am. Concentrating on the road before me, I explain that although we haven't dated for long, I know that he is the one, the only one, for me.

"Well dear, where's there's life, there's hope," she tells me with a sigh, as she looks away from me and out the window, to places I cannot yet see.

"Umm hmm," I say, agreeing with her wisdom with the nodding of my head, not knowing what she's talking about.

♥

As a child, I learned about love and affection from television, as God was as emotionally and physically distant to me as both my parents. Where did you form your first ideas of love?

Trust in the Lord with all you heart and lean not on your own understanding; in all your ways acknowledge him, and he will make your paths straight.

Proverbs 3:5, 6

May 2001

"I'm not going to have this baby if it means being told what to do for the rest of my life." I thought, closing the door behind me.

After having driven around all night to find me, Luke waited in the morning for me at my parked car outside of my girlfriend's house, where I had spent the night. When I saw him, with his stern look and crossed arms, my face crumbled in guilt and although I didn't intend to, I smiled despite it, thinking that I had shown him, but by hurting me.

"You are not a nice girl"

"I am a nice girl, just not all the time"

Up to that point, I had willingly given him all my freedom and choices, and like a petulant child, I wanted them back.

I had had enough of being serious, of the reality of a life I didn't know how to live, no matter how hard I tried, with a man I could never seem to please. I wanted to go where I felt I belonged, except that I didn't belong there either; it seemed I didn't belong anywhere, anymore.

I'm just scared, I wished for the words to say as I sat silently, my hands folded in my lap, while he continued to scold me. *Terrified in fact, of a life that will rob me of everything I love about myself, causing it all to disappear. That I will no longer be the girl with dreams and goals of more. Instead I'll lose all that I am in the role of mother, wife and personal maid, eventually ceasing to exist altogether.*

That is what scares me the most, that with motherhood, I will become less instead of more.

We broke up and I packed up my apartment and left him, not that he was sorry to see me go. I needed some time to think about who I am and the direction of my next step.

I am lead to a secluded picnic table at a calm and peaceful lake, where I write and write looking for an answer to the many questions of my heart. I write about the part of me that wonders if this child could be a beginning to the elusive "more" that I desire, that wants a real life with days more important than my nights.

The reality is I want more time to choose this life instead of having it choose me, but the truth is it did choose me and I don't yet know the reason why. I need to place my life and faith in the hands of a God that I barely understand, and trust in the bigger picture, the picture only he can see, if he does indeed exist.

Having made my choice, I begin to look forward to what my life will be, instead of back to what it once was, promising myself that all the things I want in life are still possible.

God won't give me anything I can't handle, I surmise as I close my journal, vowing to myself to focus only on the present and try my best, praying it's enough because it's all I've got.

♥

I believe this is the moment I turned my life over to the care of God, as I understood Him. What is your understanding of God?

The Lord is close to the brokenhearted and saves those who are crushed in spirit.

Psalm 34:18

July 2001

"Goodnight baby," Luke says softly, with a loving pat to my swelling abdomen before turning his back to me.

"Sorry. Goodnight to you too," he says, giving me a quick peck on the forehead, before turning away from me again, this time for the night.

But I will lay awake on my side for hours yet, my back to his, my knees curled up tightly around my growing belly looking through the large window of our shared, yet quietly divided bedroom.

Through eyes brimming with tears, I look beyond its framework of painted white, peeling squares of wood, towards the random spattering of lights set aglow against the dark blue of the summer night sky. By the light of those stars, I continue to place my faith and trust in something I cannot see or feel, when all that surrounds me is hopelessness, and I cannot remember a time I felt more alone.

The butterflies brought me back here, but they have all flown away now that I have decided to stay. What remains now is a man of duty by my side, punishing me for not being the nice girl he had thought I was by wrapping a blanket tightly around his body, to ensure the distance between us will continue, even in sleep.

I've finally given up on begging for his affection and touch, knowing it will only make him mad when I cannot control my tears as he turns his eyes and lips away from mine, realizing that it is indeed possible to feel less loved than I already was.

My heart knows it has nothing to offer that he wants, as the hot, wet tears that fill me begin their quiet slide down my cheeks, as I stare into the perfect night sky with its perfect stars asking why.

Why, when I try so hard to be the woman he wants, can he not be the man I need?

I know that I have made my choice and that with it comes this bed in which lies a man who tells me he just doesn't have it in him to care about anyone anymore. Luke has told me he wants only to support me as his friend and be a father to his child, but I stay in the hope that, as a mother, I will soon be so different that he will change his mind and we can be a family.

Every day, I gauge his mood to define my own, carrying the burden of his constant control, trying my best to create a woman he can love, the woman he had dreamed I was. I begin to wonder if there will be anything left of me by trying to love him as day after day, I feel smaller and smaller, reminding him of his mother, a woman he tells me he hates, who was always sad and tired, just like me.

This is my life now, I tell myself, giving up the fight for a life of my own, but it still isn't enough because he wants complete control over who I am; everything from what I wear to whom I speak. It is not so much what he asks of me that is the problem, but in the way that he asks it, demanding that I live by one set of rules while he lives by another, both his, that have made me begin to question his lead.

When I do speak on the telephone to the few friends I have left, either in secret or while he hovers and listens nearby, I can't make them understand why I am having this man's baby or why I don't leave him and never look back.

They simply don't see the good in him or understand him as I do, as only I can, because I have seen pictures of his heart and know of the joy that lives there, if only he would trust me with it.

For the first time in my life, I ask God directly, *"Why did you send me this man who I can love who can't love me back?"*

With closed eyes and open heart, I wait as slowly the answer comes, *You Need Each Other*, my heart hears, and although I have peace that this is true, my mind still wonders, *in what way?*

I think of my child and question if the mother that I hope for lives in me, or if the reality of failure will be too much to bear. I want so much to teach him or her not to judge, but instead to accept, love and forgive. To be so careful with his or her own heart and whom is let into it, to know it as a treasure and take good care of it, never settling for less in this life than he or she deserves. But most of all what I hope I can teach this little child of mine is to never give up, to always have faith in what cannot yet be seen.

But how, I wonder, can I teach a child what I have not yet learned myself?

♥

My self-worth and personal value was based on the love and acceptance of another person. Have you experienced codependency?

"Arise, my darling, my beautiful one, and come with me."

Song of Songs 2:10

May twenty-first, 1993

When I saw him at a party, I knew that Jacob was the most beautiful boy I had ever seen. All the girls surrounded him and judging by his looks, it was easy to see why. It was not any one thing that made him so beautiful, but every little thing that I never knew I wanted, until I saw him, that fascinated me. From afar, it was his beautiful light brown hair with just a hint of Scottish red and his well-dressed long, lean body, but upon looking closer, I saw that his real beauty laid in all his contradictions.

How his strong, manly and chiseled jaw held soft, sweet full red lips and his brilliant hazel green eyes flecked with gold, implied a secret by shyly casting downward as he spoke. Even with his apparent boredom with all the attention that he received, he seemed to have a quiet defiance of his beauty as more of a burden, rather than a blessing.

We all began to talk in the kitchen, my friends and his friend Mike, hardly noticing at all as, one by one, the people surrounding us slowly disappeared, and before long, it was just the two of us.

"Would you like a drink?"

"I don't drink."

"Ever?" I asked incredulous, as he laughed and I stared, a bit stunned. This guy was different from anyone I had ever met and I liked that, a lot.

He dropped me off last and we sat talking in the dark of his car outside my house. With nowhere to look but at the folded hands in my lap, I waited patiently for the cost of his attention, but there was none as he got my phone number, promised to call and shyly we said goodnight.

I lay in bed that night and tried not to dream of a future with someone so interesting and beautiful, not wanting to be too happy to be chosen, only to feel twice as sad when he decided he didn't want me after all.

But, two days later, he called. He chose me.

July 1993

Jacob's was the first kiss I really wanted and I waited patiently for him to get up the nerve. The summer sun set as we lay on our sides, me with one hand between my knees while the other caressed all the contradictions to the beauty upon his face.

I committed every detail of him to the memory of my heart, as my curious fingertips grazed the sharp outline of his jaw to the sweetness of his cheek, sweeping the prominent eyebrows that framed eyes of purity, my touch seeming to move the clouds that kept their golden flecks concealed.

At evening's end, lying side by side, we talked quietly about everything and nothing at all while I searched behind his eyes, reaching silently for his heart, for what I felt and what it meant. He answered my every question without ever saying a word when he cupped my face between his hands, closed his eyes and tenderly kissed me slowly from my forehead to my lips. Gently, I began to close my own.

Legs and arms entwined, we faced one another, our quiet conversation interrupted only by my periodic and delighted giggles, that filled his once plain room. His eyes and lips smiled back at me, both our spirits giddy with the change, eventually falling asleep in the same way, *changed*.

♥

I feel loved when someone spends quality time listening, affirming and/or being affectionate with me. What actions make you feel loved by another person?

And a little child will lead them.

Isaiah 11:6

November twenty-ninth, 2001

"Luke, are you awake?" I whisper, gently resting my hand on his leg in the dark of his bedroom, feeling his body move slightly beneath the covers.

"Luke," I whisper a little louder, "I think I'm going into labor. It hurts a lot."

"Go back to bed," he tells me, turning over and adding sleepily, "Don't wake me until it's serious. I have to work in the morning."

My bare feet pad their way through the kitchen, my pregnant belly protruding from my nightgown leading the way as, all alone, I find my way back to my makeshift bedroom on his sofa bed, where we had once made life by candlelight, in the living room.

Lying down, I hold my stomach and tell it that I am sorry, I am so sorry, as I try not to cry for all the different ways life should have been and try to accept it for what it is.

November thirtieth, 2001

"Wow, that is so weird," are my first motherly words, trying to grasp the enormity of creating a real live human being in my body, with my mind. He is as close to God as I have ever been, the pride and value I feel in being his mother, matched only with the knowledge that he is my son. My son.

Peace falls as my fingertips stroke the top of his head, slowly and gently, receiving this glorious new creation in my arms, with all of my heart. I silently promise him with each stroke that I will take good care of him and not to worry, that we will be just fine.

I check and make sure that he has all the necessary parts, relieved to find he is indeed as perfect as he appears and after three sleepless nights, we go back home. I am hoping for the best and, after some initial adjustment from Luke, thinking that I just might get it.

"I want to love you and I want you to love me too," Luke says exhausted, sitting with his head in his hands as I kneel at his feet, forgiving him.

I am happier than I ever thought possible to lie beside him and discuss a future together, beginning to believe again in him and in his ability to love me. Especially when I watch him with our son, named David, as Luke holds him close and consoles his cries, whispering in his ear as he dances him around the living room, to his new favorite song about a hero kissing away the pain.

♥

Conversely, without communication or affection, I feel neglected and rejected. Are there actions of another person that activate feelings of abandonment in you?

Love never fails.

1 Corinthians 13: 8

August 1993

"Can you turn this up?" I asked excitedly, hearing one of my favorite songs on the radio, as I jumped into Jacob's car and closed the door quickly behind me.

He turned up the radio, but instead of driving away, stopped to watch as my body and feet wriggled and stamped away in my seat, overcome with the beat, completely unaware of his gaze.

"You are beautiful, you know that?" he said with a shake of his head and a grin, as I gave him a quick kiss on his cheek, secretly smiling at the compliment because I wasn't trying to be beautiful.

"Awww, you guys are so cute," his friend said. She smiled sweetly as she lowered her video camera at the picnic with his friends, where we sat together holding hands and kissing every time we thought that the others had looked away.

Yet she captured us, with our faces close while we looked eye to eye and talked softly to each other. We both laughed and looked away with red faces at the sight of her camera, embarrassed at being seen by another, in a way that was reserved for only the two of us.

Later, tired from the day, I curled up on my side with my head resting lightly in his lap on the couch, as he loved me over and over again with his hand caressing my hair. With each slow, gentle stroke of his hand, my eyes gently began to close. My mind drifted away to a place where everything was safe and my heart whispered, *I love you, I love you, I love you.*

His hand lay still and heavy with the silence, resting in mid stroke upon my head, his breath slow and even, as I felt his chest slowly rise and then fall. My own body lay rigid and panicked, eyes open wide, body braced to be pushed from his lap to the floor.

My mind cringed with its own stupidity, wondering if I had indeed said aloud to him what I had only meant to think, until he leaned down, breathed me in and spoke words my heart had longed to hear.

"I love you too, Frances."

♥

This was the first time in my life I said *I love you* and heard it in return. Do you believe "love never fails" and if so, how does love never fail?

But seek first his kingdom and his righteousness, and all these things will be given to you as well.

Matthew 6:33

February 2002

"What do you mean, I *can't* go to school?"

"You need to work so we can start saving for a home for our family. We have to come first."

I say nothing as I sit sullenly across from him on the sofa in the living room, looking only at my hands in my lap, disconnecting completely from him and us, as our definitions of success collide.

But there is something I'm supposed to do, I think to myself.

All I really want is to be left alone to care for my son and am here now only out of fear of what life lies outside of this one. I know he feels the change in me as he provides the push I need in another direction, threatening the promise I made to myself beside a calm, beautiful and peaceful lake, when I remember I had felt strong enough to try, with or without him.

Now. Run.

Through the big glass windows of the coffee shop, I see him standing in line, watching me closely while he waits for our coffees, both of us tired from yet another night trapped in one of his episodes.

My body smiles and waves, but my mind races. Slowly my eyes travel from him to our silent witness, who waits happily in his car seat. Instinctively, I open the car door and jump in, slamming it behind me and driving away. When he sees me leave, he drops our coffees with a splash and begins to run at top speed behind my car.

In our house, my heart beats frantically as my shaking hands grab whatever they can find, while my car waits in our driveway. I hurry back to the car, desperate to get away. It's then that I see him.

In the reflection of my rearview mirror, I see him clutching his chest, in an attempt to catch his breath, and my eyes soften at the sight of him, weak and defeated, tugging at my heart to stop and help him one more time.

But I continue to drive away, vowing to myself never to go back, as I drive to my sister, Rebecca's, where she informs me that I can always leave him, but I won't always have the option to stay.

I return, with my head down and heart set on learning how to stay. Instead, I learn how to stay out of his way, trying to keep things, in what we call our home, from escalating, as I struggle to block out all the things he tells me I already am and am destined to be.

My spirit begins to believe again in a life that I deserve, that lies outside of this one, not wanting to give up on a life and a love that I need to believe in, knowing that if I give up on it, it may give up on me.

How did I get here? I wonder, *and how do I get away?*

♥

I know that I could not live my life happily without a higher purpose. What does it mean to you, to seek God?

"Peace I leave with you; my peace I give you."

John 14:27

March thirtieth, 2002

"I said, NOW!"

Blindly, my fingers reach for the covers of the bed, but just as they finally find them, the blankets are ripped from my hands and tossed on the floor, leaving me completely exposed on the bed. Luke orders me to get up, to once again, "talk about our relationship."

Not wanting him to wake David, I use all the energy I have left to try and sit my tired body up, dropping my legs over the edge of the bed, unable to move anymore than this.

"Frances!" he yells again so loudly that my whole body jumps, until finally, I do as I am told.

It is David's fifth month in his new world, and tonight, my lack of sleep and complete exhaustion over our constant battles have taken their toll. I realize that my true power lies in conceding defeat, instead of trying again and again to change the truth, as gradually, what once was our war, becomes solely his own. This peace within me grants me victory.

It doesn't matter to me why he does what he does, I just want him and it to stop.

Luke becomes desperate for a reaction as I let him win his war. Its then that he brings out his video camera and erratically, he begins to videotape me. Still receiving no reaction from me, except the pity I convey for him in my eyes, he continues to test my resolve.

"I've been videotaping you. Now everyone will know that you're a bad mother and I'm a good father," he says, taunting me with the camera.

Despite my best efforts not to be interested, not to play the game, I am curious about his evidence. I hold out my hands as he places the camera in them and plays me the tape, proud at the level of his intelligence.

It is shortly after he has returned home from a hard day at work, the focal point of my entire day and all its activities, making certain that everything is in near perfect order by the time he arrives home to his new family. I can hear myself busy in the kitchen, learning how to make dinner, while the video shows him, fresh from his shower, playing affectionately with David on our living room floor.

I walk into its view and sit down on the sofa, curling up my knees beneath me and talking at length, all about the little moments of my day spent with our son while he was away at work. I am careful to listen as much as I talk, asking politely about his day too, thankful that on this day, he is in a good mood, and is happy to do both.

I look at this family. *They look happy.*

I see the girl that he was trying so hard to make into some type of monster, whose only crime seemed to be that she wanted that scene to exist, and for her ignorance to last. Stunned and haunted by its image, I put the camera down slowly, to rest it on the table, no longer willing or wanting to feel the sadness of this girl anymore.

It was all just so sad, sad for him and for me. But most of all, sad for us ~ our family.

I stare down at the long grain that follows the length of his kitchen table, where we had once sat as he told me his story, when I had thought I had it in me to help him laugh and smile again. I bury my head in my hands, to hide my face from his, so he won't see that the hurt I feel in my heart, has spread all over my face.

I take my hands away from my face to look at him, in an effort to see in his eyes the reason why, but when I do, instead of his eyes, I see the cold, heartless eye of the video camera lens. He has picked it up with glee, after finally provoking a reaction from me, and is now recording and relishing my heartbreak, for his proof.

From a place of sadness within myself, my entire soul, so consumed with grief and hurt, finds a deep dark noise that begins as a slow low moan of such intensity and despair that its strength forces my head to fall back and my mouth to open wide, as an unearthly howl leaves my body. With a life and energy all its own, my soul cries out in pain.

Please don't hurt me anymore, it begs.

Make it Stop, Make it Stop, my mind screams, my head still reared back and my face contorted by the pain, looking up to where God should be.

I feel Luke cautiously backing away from me, feeling his timid shame of the winning of his war. From what seems to be very far away, I hear the soft slow click of the camera, as he closes it and lays it on the table in front of me, as a quiet offering of peace.

Using all my strength to bring my heavy head forward again, I stare in disbelief at the camera, unable to say or feel anything at all as, in a daze, I get up and stagger back to bed.

March thirty-first, 2002

"Shhh…shhhh…its okay, baby…its okay…don't cry,"

I console David as I quickly and quietly dress him, unsure if I have slept at all, careful not to wake his father.

Don't think. Don't feel. Don't think. Don't feel.

My body is on autopilot as I gather a few belongings, knowing only that I have planned to attend Easter service today at a Christian church by the name of Victory, that I have been watching in secret, every day on television.

That's as much as my mind can grasp; that today is Easter Sunday, a day of new beginnings, and we are going to church.

♥

The purpose of abuse is to gain power and control over another. What then, is the purpose of love?

All night long on my bed I looked for the one my heart loves;
I looked for him but did not find him.

Song of Songs 3:1

October 1993

I waited for Jacob in my bed, where every night he had laid with his face next to mine as our eyes begged to close. Eventually, I would turn and relax into the silent rhythm of his soft, warm breath upon my neck as my fingers laced their way through his and resting his hand upon my heart, I enjoyed the gentle, quiet peace of his embrace.

It was a calm Saturday evening now, a stark contrast to all the noise of a Halloween party the night before. Where, dressed as his Maid Marian with him as my Robin Hood, I had decided to stay with a girlfriend who called herself my best, asking me to stay with her instead of going home with him.

"Come on, stay, please. He'll forgive you," she begged.

It wasn't the first time, but it would be the last, that I would turn my back and dismiss him, as he left to drive my other friends home and again when he returned, hoping for a change of my heart and mind, feeling his eyes on me where he waited by the door to leave.

I turned my head, to softly meet his gaze from where I felt him watching me. As our eyes met, he cast his down and away, shaking his head slowly as he walked away from me, this time without looking back.

It wasn't like him not to call, He always called, I thought all the next day and night in my bedroom, surrounded by moments and memories of him, of us, as I waited for my telephone to ring.

I slid my fingertips lovingly over the soft silk of my only dress and one of my favorite moments, closing my eyes to love the way this pretty green dress he had seen in a store window, felt beneath their touch.

My face had tried hard to hide its disappointment that day, when he handed me an old crumpled paper bag with "½ dozen donuts" written in messy black marker across its front, as a gift to celebrate one of our monthly anniversaries.

"Thank you! Thank you! Thank you!" I shrieked as I hugged him with the beautiful green dress held tightly in my hands, while he laughed and hugged me back.

What was I doing that was so wrong, that no matter how hard I tried to love and be loved, it never worked? I wondered, as I closed my eyes tightly, a few tears of defeat escaping and trickling down my cheeks, landing on the silk of the dress.

I lay down upon my bed and thought of my father and how it was his fault that I didn't know how to love a man. I blamed my mother for never showing me how to keep one.

But, mostly I blamed myself because the reality was that I did not know how to love, regardless of the reasons why.

I relied on the memory of my heart, as I pictured his eyes where I had seen a secret beyond their flecks of gold, beyond a heart purer than I had ever known, to a secret that had always been kept from me.

For the very first time in my life, *I saw me.*

In the safety and calm of his eyes and love, I finally drifted off to sleep, waking to find those eyes staring at me in a way that I had never known, as if they had never known me at all.

"Jay," I whispered in a breath, rising to open my arms and heart, hoping for him to do the same, pleased as he lay with his head in my lap and trusted me one more time with the silent tears of his little boy heart. But then, just as quickly as he had appeared, he disappeared, taking with him his tear-stained cheeks and stealing away from me as he ran out the door.

That was love. Anyone I let see me will love me just like that, I thought as my heart remained wide awake, while my body curled up and waited for sleep.

♥

I let down the first person that ever showed me love and I hated myself for it. How does one learn how to love?

Do not let the sun go down while you are still angry, and do not give the devil a foothold.

Ephesians 4: 26, 27

May 2002

"I'm not your therapist, or your girlfriend, and you are not my problem anymore!"

I hate him. I hate him. I hate him. I hate everything about him. I hate how the phone rings when it's him, always when I'm busy, to the sound of his voice when I pick it up. I hate the sight, smell and the very thought of him. I hate him. I even hate him for making me hate him, having never hated anyone before in my life.

He is not doing well, which is to be expected, as he makes threats and then promises about what he will and will not do in terms of being a father. Truthfully, I don't really care what he does or doesn't do. I don't care about him at all, and a part of me believes that if he does do all that he threatens he might, we may all be better off.

Today is a bad day, and not all are. Some days, I have the patience to listen to him and treat him as the eight-year-old boy I see in him, constantly carrying the burden, safety and power of being right, because he is always wrong and at times it's as exhausting as raising another child.

However, now that I no longer want his love, I begin to approach our situation strictly as business. A business in which I am manager, CEO and president of all operations, because I know exactly what I'm doing. I've read books, lots of them.

The reality is that I have something that he wants, a relationship with his son and he has something I want, a relationship for my son with his father, and one way or the other, we both have to figure out a way to get what we want.

The only proof I need of the man he could be is to see him in the way that my little boy does. David's bright blue eyes light up as his tiny arms stretch and legs pump away at the excitement and anticipation of his father's love. I see that same light of love and joy in his father's eyes with the sight of his son; it is when they look the most alike.

Unfortunately, instead of the situation becoming easier with each passing day, reality gets harder and more permanent. I am determined to fix my life and yet, the receiver that I slam down on Luke's ear, is the very same one I want to pick up to call him back because I miss the feeling of being loved, even a little bit, even if at his very best, he never loved me very well.

It just seems such a monumental task to start a new relationship with anyone else, especially if I am to choose that person with the wisdom of God, when I do not yet have such wisdom. Sometimes I just want someone, anyone, to just know me, to really see me and that seems the most monumental task of all.

♥

My love for him was as intense as my hate for him. How is love and hate the same and different?

Do not arouse or awaken love until it so desires.

Song of Songs 3:5

October 2002

"Look who it is!" my sister, Rebecca says loudly, looking again and again from Dracula's face to mine.

I look blankly at Dracula, with his long black cape and silly fake white teeth smiling knowingly at me dressed in my cowgirl costume of faded blue jeans, white t-shirt and white straw hat to match.

My eyes travel over the complete picture of Dracula, and then slowly begin to focus in on his details. His hair, a beautiful light brown with just a hint of Scottish red. His face with a strong, chiseled jaw. Then, finally, his eyes, smiling and kind, with those tiny little flecks of gold speckled on a brilliant hazel green. It was then that I really saw him, without him ever saying a word.

"It's Jacob!" my sister squeals with delight.

"Close your mouth, dear," she adds.

Silently, I obey her command, but my eyes remain wide open, in complete disbelief that I am seeing my precious Jacob, having imagined every detail of this moment for so many years. Now that it has finally arrived, I am powerless to think of a single word to say.

"You look really good," Jacob says, cocking his head to the side, his eyes sweeping me from head to toe in the middle of the crowd of people dressed for Halloween. But, it was he who looked good, better than my dreams would allow my heart to see, time having turned him from a sweet boy into a gentle man.

"This is my first Halloween party since..." he offers, his eyes looking mischievously into mine as I return his smile with my eyes.

Say something, say anything, my mind whispers.

"I had a son." I finally blurt out.

"Really? I have two children..."

"Yes, I know. Hannah and Riley." I interrupt and then am immediately embarrassed that I have, by the way he looks at me with that sparkle in his eye and his silly grin.

"Did you get my letter?" I feel safe enough to ask, noting the absence of a ring on his left hand.

"Yes, but I didn't read it. I just don't need to read something like that right now," he replies with a heavy sigh, for the first time casting his eyes down, and then looking anxiously up, to scan the entire room for the mother of his children, a life begun shortly after the ending of ours.

"Oh. Right. Yes. Of course. I understand," I stumble and stammer, searching for the right words to say, thinking that the right words had all been in my letter sent shortly after David's birth.

A letter from my heart that he never read, I realize as I feel that same heart sink in front of a man I hadn't known since I was a girl and he was a boy. My eyes grow dark and cold as I stare blankly at him before looking completely past him and over his shoulder. All I see next is the countless bottles of liquor lining their way sporadically across the kitchen counter silently promising to heal my broken heart.

"Excuse me," I say to him, moving myself away from him and towards them.

The next morning, I lay horrified as the events of the evening flashed before my closed eyes. Me—drinking, drinking, drinking—yelling at my sister, *Jacob loves me, NOT HER!* -

Sitting on the steps outside the party, studying his face, the face that I remember and love with all of my being, his lips so close I could feel his warm breath on mine. I couldn't help it. The temptation was too great. I tried to kiss him. He pushed me gently away and I staggered back and fell to the ground where I watched as he left me once again.

The last thing I remember was leaning against the door as I watched him dance with the mother of his children, who didn't even seem to want to dance with him, wishing that it was me.

I wanted to show him how much I changed, but instead, I showed him how much I had stayed the same and I hated myself for it. For the first time in my life, I thought, *I think I have a drinking problem*. Unfortunately, it wouldn't be the last.

♥

Until I addressed my problems with alcohol, I would never have a healthy relationship with others, or myself in my life. What is self-love to you?

"This is the way; walk in it."

Isaiah 30:21

October 2003

Why are you letting me be so lonely for so long? I silently ask a God I hadn't spoken to at all in a couple of years, having decided that I didn't think much of his plan so far, instead choosing to believe in myself and make some plans of my own.

Unable to feel anything at all, I fall back on my bed and stare blankly at the ceiling while David is away with his father, living a life completely independent of his mother.

The phone rings and it is my sister, Rebecca, catching me in my moment of weakness and inviting me to join a twelve-step program with her at her church. Something I have absolutely no interest in attending, remembering the last time I was at church.

"Could you please pray for me to have the strength to stay?" I had pleaded.

"We'll pray for you to know the right thing to do," the peaceful-looking man and woman offering prayer that Easter Sunday had said quietly, as they closed their eyes and wrapped their arms around me and my newborn son.

"Well, you can figure these things out now or wait twenty years, like I have, to have a healthy relationship," Rebecca not-so-gently suggests and begrudgingly, I agree to take a small step in a different direction.

"Strong like an oak with petals slowly falling and dying one by one at the foot of its trunk," I tell the circle of women at the church, utterly horrified that I almost begin to cry describing myself as a tree.

"Let go and Let God," they say in unison and I nod my head in agreement.

What did that mean? How does one let go and let God? Let Him do what? To me, letting go sounded to me like letting yourself go, the phrase itself implying a lack of ambition and drive. To me, letting go looked like giving up and I couldn't give up on me, no matter what.

I want some proof of God, if I am to change my ways for Him. I want some kind of sign.

Driving home, I hear a song play softly on the radio and turn it up to hear its words over the rhythm of the rain. It breathes the sound of hope in me, singing about love and who you are in the eyes of it.

I begin to think back, instead of always blindly pushing forward, starting to remember as far back as my memory will allow, of life before my son, the life that seemed to completely disappear with his birth.

So simple and selfish it once was, I remember, barely recalling the anxiety and discomfort of my constant need for more, of what I was never sure, but always wanting more of something of which I did not have enough. It still existed, this need for more, but it was different now, because now I wanted more not only for me, but for us.

"That was for Frances..." The deejay says as I pull up to my building complex. I stop and stare in shock at the radio in my car and hurriedly grab my keys, without bothering to lock the doors, to run inside and call Rebecca.

"It was so weird, Rebecca, the song and the words. I started thinking about everything and then, and then, my name came on over the radio! It was dedicated to me! It was a sign!" I tell her excitedly.

"So... what exactly am I supposed to do now?"

♥

Today, I think of letting go as the words of the Serenity Prayer suggest: God, grant me the serenity to accept the things I cannot change, the courage to change the things I can and the wisdom to know the difference." What does the phrase "Let Go and Let God" mean to you?

Free yourself from the chains on your neck, O captive Daughter of Zion.

Isaiah 52:2

June 2004

"We have a special treat this evening, ladies and gentlemen, a first-timer and you all know how much we love those…" the announcer says as I wait where my spirit has lead me, behind the dark velvet curtain of a comedy club. *All I can be is me,* I tell myself as I slow my breathing, trying to focus only on what I have come here prepared to do.

I do not care what happens if I fail, for I have failed before and always learned something. My real fear is what happens if I succeed: that is what scares me the most, as that is something I have yet to do.

"So, please, put your hands together and give a warm welcome to Frances Stone."

I give the announcer's hand a firm shake before he leaves, wanting to hold on, but learning to let go, as I step out into an abyss that holds what looks like a thousand faces. My body gravitates toward where the tall, gleaming silver microphone stands beneath the shining spotlight. I take a deep breath and prepare to speak.

"My boss thinks I'm a very negative person. I'm not. I'm a very positive person. I am positive that I hate him, and I am positive that I hate his stupid job."

All the feelings I have kept inside because they are not right to feel, to think, all spill out of me as I ask out loud and without apology, *Why? Why do people do the things they do, in the way that they do them? Why? Why? Why?*

The mask I wear in my day-to-day life that says I'm fine and good, no matter how I really feel, falls away and I am free in a way that I have never known, to be completely myself as I remember exactly who that is. I start to feel bigger and bigger than I really am and then, just as quickly as it had begun, it ends. Then, there is a horrible sound in its place.

Silence.

Speak. Speak. I urge myself. But I can't. I can't think of a single thing to say as the thousand faces that a moment ago appeared friendly, are all at once menacing now, watching and waiting for me to fail, to lose and give up.

I sigh deeply, cast my eyes to the ground and bow my head at the tall, silver microphone. I hear a voice I know very well, the voice that hates me, that wants to see me fail, that doesn't want me to try again.

What are you doing? Why did you think you could do this? Who do you think you are?

I am no one. I am nothing.

Give up!

Clap. Clap. Clap. Clap.

From the dark, far corner of the room, I hear the impossibly slow, loud and methodical echo of two hands coming together to deliver exactly what I need, at the exact time that I need it, without me even having to ask. Drawing on their strength, I slowly raise my head to meet the eyes that wait for me, take a deep breath and try again.

The once steady green light is now blinking a flashing red, to warn me that I have gone past my allotted time, still feeling that I have so much more I need to say, but not quite knowing what it is yet. Blissfully, I blow a kiss to the crowd, feeling as though I am floating on air, and exit the stage through the dark velvet curtain.

That's it! That's what I've been looking for my whole life! I whisper to myself, leaning lightly against the curtain, not wanting to leave it behind, my eyes shut in relief because I have finally found what I am supposed to do. At the very least, I am extremely close.

♥

The truth will set you free. What do you hide from others that keeps you from being your authentic self?

"For everyone born of God overcomes the world. This is the victory that has overcome the world—our faith."

1 John 5:4

August 2004

"I'm not here to fit in. I'm here because I don't," I tell one of my fellow comedians, one of the many friends I've made here, where I have begun to laugh and smile once again.

We move again, this time to a beautiful one bedroom apartment with a gorgeous view of the city, that I can barely afford, but think that soon I will, now that all my dreams will come true.

When David is at his father's, I eat and sleep comedy, spending my entire day thinking about five minutes of it, the five minutes I might have a chance to be seen and heard on stage that night. I write my bits and routines constantly, always thinking, thinking, thinking of my next performance, my very next chance to be me.

Through stand-up comedy, I begin to see the world in a different way, as I quietly observe and dissect every moment of it. My mind is constantly asking why, yet never fully appeased with the reason it's given, always leaving it with yet another question and answer, following yet another reason to ask why, never willing to accept the explanation that it simply, is.

"Look, Mommy, I'm broken," my now three-year-old David says, holding up his truck for Mommy to see.

No, you're not - you're perfect. I say softly, my hand gently tousling his blonde hair as I lean down to give him a kiss, a Mommy kiss, the kind that makes everything better.

It is me that is the broken one.

Having endlessly searched my conflicted heart, I know within it that I must walk away, but don't know to where, or to what as alcohol begins to beckon to me daily, forever offering its temporary escape.

October 2004

"Are you sure you can afford this?" the teacher of yet another self-help group, this one of the artistic variety, asks.

"I can't afford not to," I reply, looking her straight in the eye.

I begin to write. Every morning, I write. I write and write, until it hurts to write. Then I cry.

"I need you to come pick up these boxes and get them out of my attic," my mother says firmly to me, over the telephone.

They are boxes of my old journals, ones I had not seen in years. I leafed through them, amused at first by my ramblings, and then I began to read their words more closely, more intently, trying to learn something about the girl who wrote them.

I see how many years of her life she has been doing exactly the same things, in exactly the same ways, and how much of that time was spent searching for "The One" when it was the idea of a perfect love that she loved, not a real love, with the commitment and sacrifice it required. Page after page, I'm shown how endlessly she has tried to get what she wants, when truly, she never did, because she was always so focused on what she could get, instead of what she could give.

It was all here, in black, blue and sometimes angry red ink, whatever I could find to write, to speak. Me. My Self. How and when I learned to hide. I see how much of my life has been spent hiding in these pages, in the only place where I felt safe to ask the questions of my heart and have my voice be heard.

In that moment, at the very bottom of the box, I see a carefully folded piece of paper and gingerly pick it up, to hear a loving voice from my past.

I open it carefully, closing my eyes softly and breathing in deeply the spirit of what I hold at my fingertips. It is an old love letter from Jacob, full of sweet nothings that meant everything, in his boxy childish handwriting I remember so well.

"Life is a story. Make sure yours ends well," the note says.

I think of my story and the story of my mother and father, which I have begun tentatively to write, having noticed some similarities between their story and my own, revealing my own mother to me, in a new and different light.

I see how easy it was to choose to be a mother with a house, husband and career, the things I had convinced myself motherhood required, when those were the things a mother always stood to lose, nearly forgetting about the one thing that mattered most, the one thing a mother couldn't live without, faith.

For without it, would she have chosen me?

The note slips through my fingers, falling slowly into the box that lay empty now beside me, loose-leaf papers and assorted colored books strewn about where I sit, stunned by what has been revealed to me on my living room floor. By the time I am finished reading, I see myself in a way I never have before. I see the part I can change. I see how I can end well and it makes me feel something I have not felt in a very long time.

I feel free. I feel so free.

♥

Self-awareness is the beginning of change. Do you see the part in your own story that you can change — to end well?

If you forgive anyone, I also forgive him. And what I have forgiven—if there was anything to forgive—I have forgiven in the sight of Christ for your sake, in order that Satan might not outwit us. For we are not unaware of his schemes.

2 Corinthians 2:10, 11

January twentieth, 2005

"Daddy's asleep, Mommy. Daddy's asleep."

"Let's go. Let's go. Come on, honey. Let's go." I say, grabbing my car keys as I quickly pick him up in my arms to rush us out the door.

It is late, dark and past his bedtime. We were waiting for his father to arrive for a late dinner to discuss scheduling, but I had been so busy writing and puttering around the house that I hadn't noticed at all that hours had passed since he was scheduled to arrive.

I phoned again and again. No answer.

It wasn't like him not to call. He always called.

But I don't think of any of this now, only this feeling that overwhelms me that something has happened, something bad. I just want to drive to his house and see if his car is there. If it is, then we're in trouble.

"Please Lord, let me be wrong. Please. Please. I just want to be wrong," I plead, my hands tightly gripping the steering wheel, instantly aware of all the times I had insisted on being right.

I arrive at his house and see his car is there. I see it, but I can't go in. I can handle whatever has happened, but I just don't want to see anymore. I don't want to see any more pain. I fumble with my cell phone as I drive away, not sure where I am going, but knowing I must get away.

"Helen?" my voice quivers as it asks, having phoned his mother.

"Can I pick you up? Something has happened. I'll explain when I get there."

She says yes and when I arrive I am nearly in hysterics.

"I know it's true. I know it. I know it." I notice how she is looking at me like I am crazy, but I can't stop the flood of feelings that overwhelm me.

I try to compose myself, try to breathe calmly in and out to regain control, but its no use, instead, I hear a voice, a voice that conveys how I really feel, not how I should. It is small, quiet and full of fear. It is my own.

"I can feel it. I can feel it *in my heart*." as all at once tears wash down my cheeks, my eyes pleading with hers, my hand clutching at my chest where my heart lies beneath.

January twentieth, 2005

"I'm glad you're not dead," I say, opening the door wide, allowing him to step inside my apartment. I wrap my arms around him while his own lay motionless at his sides as we, quickly and awkwardly, share our very first hug, in a very long time.

He shakes his head as if to laugh, while I motion with my hand for him to have a seat in the living room. He sits down, hesitant and skeptical of this new me who doesn't need to scream to be heard, watching me closely and tentatively, to see what has suddenly changed.

With him on one couch and me on the other, everything feels different as we begin to talk quietly, suddenly both aware of the possibility of being allies instead of enemies, being for one another, instead of against.

"Guess you'll be meeting someone soon," he says, seeing the softer side to me again. I don't answer him. I don't know what to say.

"Don't take him away from me when you do, okay?" he asks quietly.

"You're a good father, Luke." I say sincerely.

As the mother of his child, I had never said that to him before, that he was a good father, that he was a good anything. Instead I was forever pointing out what he was doing wrong, instead of anything he was doing right.

"I didn't do anything wrong," he had said so long ago, and if that were true, how great his pain must have been, with no way to prove his love.

His pain was not about me. It was not mine to carry. It was neither mine to judge, nor mine to judge how he carried it. I could see it. I could feel it. But I didn't have to live it. He did. How much he would want someone else to feel his pain, someone other than himself, to show how much his heart hurt, without ever having to say the words.

It hurts.

Within this space, him seated on one couch and me on the other, there is this feeling of peace and understanding of everything that makes us different, but also of the one thing that makes us very much the same; our need to love and be loved.

The love we have for our son is a love that we share; a love that doesn't fight, it forgives; that doesn't hurt, it heals; that doesn't leave, it looks to learn; that gains its strength not by seeking power, but by seeking peace; that is not about being right, but about doing what's right; a love that doesn't look down or across, instead, it just makes us look up and keep looking up.

"I'm a writer, you know. I know that you don't believe in me, but I think I'm supposed to tell our story. I think that's what I'm supposed to do."

"I know you're a writer and I do believe in you, just not in the way that you want."

"I remember your poems," he adds, slowly and cautiously sharing his heart.

"I remember *you*," he says, meeting my eyes, revealing to me my place in it.

With this, I turn my head from him and look up and away, my hand falling over my eye and then sliding roughly down my cheek, trying hard to hide the big tear that falls from a heart that is so touched that he ever knew or saw me at all, thinking that, *perhaps as little as he did love me was as much as he could.*

♥

Forgiveness is the end of one story and the beginning of another. Is there anyone for you to forgive, to begin a new story?

God is love.

1 John 4:16

January twenty-first, 2005

What is this feeling? I know this feeling. I think to myself, walking home from the last bus, my second-hand car having finally given up on me, when I gave up on fixing it.

It is Friday night. David is at his father's for the night and I am again by myself, but tonight, do not feel quite so all alone. My steps are slow and easy, without the need to rush, as I think about my day while the cool night wind blows softly against my cheek.

All day long, I was paid to be me, no matter who everybody else was going to be, enjoying my day consumed by one single question, a question that I had yet to consider: *How can I help?*

As I walk, my head is up and I look people in the eye, giving them a small, friendly smile and a quick nod of my head as we pass one another on the street, unable to help myself from sharing this smile within my eyes and on my lips.

What is this feeling?

I try to analyze it with every step I take closer to home, turning it over and over again in my mind, but still can't quite put my finger on what it could be. It is as though everything about me is no longer wrong, but somehow mysteriously right, that everything about me is just as it should be, that I am wonderfully made and perfectly me. Finally, I reach the door to my apartment, put the key in its lock and as I turn the key, it finally comes to me. I remember.

This is love. I feel loved. I think as the key clicks in the lock, opening the door.

Yes. That's it. I feel loved. I realize, pleased to have solved the riddle as I carry on, happily putting away the contents of my day, as if this is a normal feeling, one that I feel all the time, not one that I haven't felt in years.

In the bathroom, splashing warm water on my face, I look up briefly and am startled and surprised by the reflection of the woman who looks back at me. I had looked at her almost every single day of her life, but never before had I seen her look in exactly this way as I hold her gaze, examining her closely for what is different.

The shame, rejection and *not good enough* that had always seemed to color and shape my face was gone, as though by magic, and in its place, a glow, as though I am lit up from the inside out.

I turn the water off, dry my face with a towel, and stop to look at her just one more time. I begin to walk back to the kitchen, when as I do, I am overwhelmed by this feeling like a wave of love, my knees buckling beneath the experience, leaving my body a crumpled heap on my kitchen floor.

Loved. Forgiven. Right here. Right now. Loved. Not for where I'm going. Not for who I'll be. For who I am. For where I am. Loved. Through it. Through all of it. To be free from it. Loved. So that I may love and be loved. Absolutely. Unconditionally. Loved.

God, Mary and Jesus. I feel them everywhere in this room and within my heart, so much so, it scares me to death.

Am I Mary? Is my son Jesus? I wonder, thinking that it has finally happened; I have completely lost my mind. Until this overwhelming sense of peace and calm tells me different.

Mary in every mother. Jesus in every child.

In me. Mary lives in me.

I crawl into bed that evening, putting my head to the pillow in the middle of the bed where I sleep alone, yet feeling as though there is someone or something right beside me and all around me, that has traveled the longest road, the road from my head all the way to my heart. Where they meet, I can hear a voice that I know is God and once he starts talking, he won't stop. He has so much to say:

You are not alone. I am with you. Do not be afraid. Every need will be met. You are safe. Trust in me. Believe in me. Follow me.

Tonight, I put every problem and worry of what tomorrow may bring into God's loving hands as a sweet, tender smile crosses my lips. My every breath is deep and slow as my eyes gently shut and with a mind clear and at rest, I sleep like a child, just like a baby.

♥

I thought love was a pretty green dress made of a fine silk that twirled all around me as I walked, because it was the one thing in my life that I could touch, see and feel as proof of a time when I was loved. Until one night, I felt something so true within my heart and mind, that defied all things logical, causing me to stop, turn around and walk a different way.

Thy will be done.

♥

How is God love? What doors could open to you and your life if you were to believe in this love?

About The Author

Frances Stone is a single mother of three beautiful children, Co-Host of Talk Recovery Vancouver, studying to be a Registered Professional Counselor, living in Vancouver, BC, Canada.

CPSIA information can be obtained
at www.ICGtesting.com
Printed in the USA
LVOW07s2009180817
545558LV00001B/1/P